The Two of Us Are One

How to Ensure a Successful Relationship from a Couple Who Were Together for 50 Years

By Ann Steffen

THE TWO OF US ARE ONE
HOW TO ENSURE A SUCCESSFUL RELATIONSHIP FROM A COUPLE
WHO WERE TOGETHER FOR 50 YEARS

Copyright Ann Steffen, 2018

ISBN: 978-0-692-14826-6

Cover design by Rob Bignell
Cover photos of Ronnie and Ann in early 1970s (gold frame)
and Ronnie, TV reporter Boyd Huppert, and Ann in
October 2015 (red frame)

Manufactured in the United States of America
First printing June 2018

For Ronnie

Contents

Introduction

T his is dedicated to the love of my life, my husband and best friend, Ronald (Ronnie) Steffen. We spent many years together as friends, lovers, and husband and wife sharing the good times and the bad, the tough times and the fun times of which there were many. Unfortunately, he had to leave, not by his choice, but he is not – or will he ever be – forgotten by me. He is probably thinking, as he said through the years, "you are going to meet someone, go on with your life and forget all about me," but it isn't going to happen. When you have been with the one person who is best for you, there isn't any thought of going on with someone else. He will always be with me but just in different ways.

Our story may be looked at as rather strange, which maybe it was, but it was very special, and I wouldn't have given it up for anything. Perhaps the following qualities of a successful relationship helped keep us together:

Compatibility

Discover each other's likes and dislikes. Know that each of you can't have everything your own way. Be flexible.

Give and Take

Do what the other one would like to do. Each of you should express what you want.

Honesty and Trust

Without honesty and trust between two people there is nothing. No matter whether it is in your working lives, social lives, or daily lives, you probably won't stay together if one of you is deceitful or lacks a firm belief in the other's reliability.

Faithfulness to Each Other

Despite outside influences, being faithful to one another is extremely important. Even if the influences are parents or friends, you have to decide with who your loyalty lies.

Enjoy and Cherish Time Together During the Good Times

There will be many events in your relationship that will be important to both of you. These events should bring the two of you closer together and make your relationship even more meaningful.

Learn and Grow from the Hard Times

There will be times through the years that prove to be very difficult but learn from them and grow. These are the times that will test your relationship – hold it together, and you'll make your relationship even more meaningful.

Know the End Will Come

Events will arise, such as the failing health of one of you, in which that person becomes more dependent. Those are the times that truly test a relationship.

If each of you commit to these qualities, you have a good chance of a lifelong love. Ronnie and I did this, and we were together 50 years, so it can work. If you feel that your partner is worth it, you have to put some work and effort into your relationship. In the end, you will be more than happy that you did.

So, on with the story of our enduring love.

Chapter 1
The Beginning

The backgrounds of two people are the beginning of their life together. There may be strong similarities and then there may be strong differences in their backgrounds. But the melding of the backgrounds of two people help to either bring them closer together or push them apart.

This is a true story of meeting a man and falling in love, a love that would last forever and beyond. We were together for 50 years but on August 12, 2016 I lost the love of my life. It has been and still is harder than anything I have ever experienced. He used to say he thought we were closer that any two people and I agree. You don't get over something like that in a few months and I am prepared that I will never get over it, get used to it maybe but never over it. Hopefully by the end of this story it will be clear how and why both of us felt this way.

This would be a good time to give a history of our backgrounds. Both of us were only children. Ronnie was born in St. Paul, Minnesota, August 17, 1929. His father owned a neighborhood grocery store near downtown Minneapolis at that time and that was the beginning of Ronnie's life in grocery stores.

One day when Ronnie was about 2 or 3 years old he was sitting outside in front of the store when a dog came along. The dog came right over to him, Ronnie put his arms around the dog and from then on that was his best friend, Pal. They did try to find the owner of the dog but to no avail so Pal did end up being his dog. If I remember correctly, Pal was a black and white English cocker spaniel.

A little while later his family moved to St. Paul, to an area along the Mississippi River that the family called "the jungle." Both Pal and Ronnie had wonderful times there. Ronnie's grandmother, Jen, had two small houses there which really were no more than shacks but then it was the depression. Ronnie and his folks lived in one house and Jen had the other one. Ronnie was very close to his grandmother, thought the world of her as did she of him. She had a drawer full of records that he would play when at her house, which may have been the start of his love of music as well as growing up with his folks and other relatives singing when they would get together.

Where they lived was at the bottom of a steep hill below Shepard Road. One winter Ronnie smoothed out the snow, poured water on the snow and when it had frozen he had his own ski slope. He made his own skis with metal rims from barrels and would go sailing down the hill almost to the river. The area was actually a paradise for a young boy with a good imagination and he did have an imagination. He loved to make things and create his own fun.

One summer day, Ronnie and Pal were outside watching a couple of fellows who were probably in the early 20s digging for worms by the river. They had a very colorful way of talking, "Look at the f*** worm", it was like that with just about everything they said. Well, to a little boy that sounded like real grownup talk so when he got home and his mother asked him what he would like for lunch he replied, "Anything f*** is fine." She couldn't believe what he said, asked where he heard it and impressed on him that he wasn't to use that word again which he didn't.

There was an elderly man who lived next door who taught Ronnie about growing flowers and helped him plant his own garden. This stuck with him all his life and years later he had the most terrific garden in the back of the house where they were living in Minneapolis.

When Ronnie was young, around 6 years old, his father was transferred by General Mills to Chicago. The three of them, his mother (Mary), his father (Arthur or Art) and Ronnie lived in an old stone 3-story stone house that had been divided into apartments in South Chicago. Pal couldn't go with to Chicago so he stayed with Jen. Unfortunately, his aunt's husband, who was a terrible person, took Pal to the University of Minnesota and sold him for experiments. That broke Ronnie's heart when he found out and Jen was furious because it happened when she was not home.

There was a grade school across the street from where they lived, Holy Cross, where Ronnie went to school. He enjoyed sports and spent much of his spare time practicing baseball, football and basketball, excelling in all but particularly baseball and football. In fact, one of the priests at Holy Cross, Father Shean, who had been a former professional baseball player with the Pittsburgh Pirates but had to give it up due to an arm injury, took Ronnie under his wing, helping him with his sports. Eventually the priest told him he could help get him a football try-out with Notre Dame.

Unfortunately Ronnie didn't get the encouragement and support at home to pursue this path. Since Ronnie has been gone, I did find a picture of the basketball team from Holy Cross with him in the picture as is Father Shean. Ronnie thought a great deal of him.

After graduating from Holy Cross, Ronnie went to several high schools including Hyde Park, where celebrity Steve Allen went, De La Salle and Mount Carmel. He didn't go to De La Salle too long because it was more in the area of north Chicago and he had to take the "L" train which took a lot of time nor did he stay at Hyde Park very long as he did not like the school. While at these schools he participated in baseball and football, particularly. Over the years he practiced all the time until he became exceptionally good. I think it was at De La Salle, but could have been one of the other schools, the coaches couldn't believe what he could do. He could kick the ball almost the length of the field. It is possible that with his talent he could have gotten an athletic scholarship to Notre Dame. Knowing him and what he could do, it is not inconceivable that eventually he could have become a professional football player.

His life in Chicago wasn't all sports. He did work and he worked hard for a young boy. One of his jobs was working in the Produce Department at the A & P grocery store. He helped unload trucks, did stocking and would help customers with questions. Mind you, he is somewhere around 12 to 14 years old at the time. Of course, in those days kids could start working at a younger age and he actually looked older than he was, he was bigger and taller than a lot of the boys and, probably because of his intent interest in sports, he had the build of an older boy.

Other jobs he had included helping move furniture, working on the loading docks unloading trucks at a trucking company and calcimining apartments. He and another boy, who was related to the trucking company owner, worked on the docks unloading the trucks. The workers were supposed to be union workers so when the union people came around Ronnie and the other boy had to take off until they were gone. All these jobs were geared more for an adult than a young teenager but he did them, working all summer and still finding time in between or in the evenings for his sports.

He had one experience that helped to somewhat change the course of his life. Holy Cross had something like a canteen in the basement where people could go to have something to eat and socialize and a bowling alley where he worked at one time setting pins. Well, one evening Ronnie and some of the other boys were sitting out in front on those low iron rails that ran along sidewalks. A man came out who Ronnie said was around 20 or 21 years old. He was looking for his truck which wasn't there, apparently someone moved it. He figured some of the kids did it but, of course, no one would admit to it. Apparently since Ronnie was the biggest of the boys, he picked on Ronnie who had nothing to do with it nor did he know where the truck was. Anyway, the man, Al, had steel rings on all his fingers and started hitting Ronnie, primarily in the face. Ronnie's friend Harry kept yelling at Al to leave him alone, that he was hurting him, none of the other boys tried to defend him. Finally Al quit. By that time Ronnie's face was bleeding. He didn't want to go home looking like that so Harry took him to his house. Harry's mother asked what had happened and they told her. After cleaning up, Ronnie went home knowing his mother would be shocked to see him like that, and he was right.

His dad was working evenings then. When he came home, saw Ronnie and found out what happened, he told him they were going to a gym the next day. It turned out it was a boxing gym owned and run by former professional world bantam weight boxing champion Johnny Coulan. When Johnny saw Ronnie's face, he knew right away why they were there. That was the beginning of Ronnie's boxing lessons. He was probably the youngest one there. He enjoyed the lessons and being around the fighters, a few who were professional. Johnny took a liking to Ronnie. After he finished his boxing training, he put the word out that he was ready for Al but he never showed up. Like his love for the other sports, this stayed with him all his life. I still can't figure out why his mother and dad never reported it to the police since Al was an adult and assaulted a minor.

Through the years they lived in Chicago, relatives would come to visit. His grandmother, Jen, would come and stay for quite a while which made Ronnie very happy. They would go to movies together as well as walking through a large cemetery not too far away. His mother's sister, Margaret, came to live with them for a few years while her husband was stationed in England during World War II. Ronnie's uncle Mike and his two children, Donna and Donald, came to live in Chicago. Mike worked for the railroad and they lived in the same building as Ronnie and his folks so the kids were with them when Mike was working and if he had to travel out of town. Another person who would visit was his uncle John who was also in the service at that time and would come to visit when he had leave. John was somewhat of an idol to a young Ronnie.

When the war ended, Margaret's husband returned after he was discharged and they headed back to Minneapolis. In the summer of 1946 Ronnie, Donna, Donald, his mother and dad also moved back to the Twin Cities. It was not uncommon in those days that if you went to school in another state to be put back a year when you started school in Minnesota and that's what happened with Ronnie. He started at Mechanic Arts High School in St. Paul, which, like so many things, is no more. In those days it was considered a good school with Roy Wilkins, head of the NAACP at one time, being a former graduate.

Sports was again a part of his school career at Mechanic Arts. It was kind of funny because my mother and father graduated from Mechanic Arts as did one of my mother's sisters. One of the teachers Ronnie had was a teacher my mother had so you know she was no kid. In those years you had to go to school in the area you lived in. Well, after they had been back from Chicago for a couple years, they moved in a more southwest area of St. Paul which meant Ronnie was in a different school district. He never changed his address because there was only six months left until he graduated and he wanted to finish at Mechanic Arts. Somehow the school system found out about the move and he had to transfer to Monroe High School where he graduated.

Since returning from Chicago, his father bought a grocery store in the area they moved to. After Ronnie's graduation, his dad moved to a couple of other stores in the same general area and Ronnie worked in the stores. During this time, which was the early 1950s, he started getting draft notices. He finally decided rather than be drafted into the Army he would enlist in the Marine Corps. His main reason was that if he should be sent to Korea and was killed, he heard the Marines would always bring the body back. So on March 27, 1952 he left for Camp Pendleton in California. The train trip out there was less than ideal and he really wasn't prepared for what he got into when arriving at Pendleton.

On one occasion an officer came in their barracks, rather late in the evening. With all the men standing at attention by their bunks, the officer walked back and forth asking, at times, rather dumb questions. If he didn't like the answer he got, the soldier found out in no uncertain terms. Once he came to Ronnie, asked a question which he answered but didn't say "Sir" at the end of the answer. That didn't set well so Ronnie got a punch in the stomach. He bent over slightly, regained his composure, stood up looking the officer right in the eye. After a few minutes, the officer walked away and they never bothered him again. Unfortunately, others were not so lucky.

The training was very rigorous but for a good reason, preparing the men for when they would be sent to Korea. Periodically Ronnie would get notices of his upcoming transfer to Korea. He decided he had to be somewhat careful about how well he did since on the firing range he was rated as sharpshooter. That would get him to Korea sooner rather than later.

Around April of 1953, or maybe earlier, he got sick with what he thought was a cold. When it didn't get any better and, in fact, was getting worse, he reported to sick bay. He ended up in the Naval Hospital in San Diego. At first they thought he had tuberculosis but then ruled that out. It took a long time before they knew what he had. Turned out it was valley fever, medical term for it is coccidioidomycosis. It is a fungus that a person can get in the San Joaquin Valley in California which was where they had been for part of their training. When he went into the service, he weighed between 185 and 200 pounds, after he had been in the hospital for a while he was down to the 139. By the time he was well enough to be discharged from the hospital, it was too close to the time of his discharge so transfer overseas wasn't going to happen – thank goodness.

Following discharge from the Marines and returning to St. Paul, Ronnie started college. He started at Hamline University. After a while, he got the idea to go into law so he began at William Mitchell Law School but after a year decided that wasn't what he wanted to do. He then began at Macalester College. His major was education, particularly English and business. He got his degree in 1959. He continued with some additional credits and eventually did his student teaching at Washington High School in St. Paul. In about 1963 he accepted a job at, of all places, Mechanic Arts High School where he had attended. It was an inner city school with some rather tough students but he was able to deal with them and they came to like him very much.

In later years he did substitute teaching for several years with two years of long term substituting at Harding High School. In the 1980s he took a federal civil service test and got a job with the Veterans Administration at Fort Snelling which eventually lead to transferring to the Post Office at the same location. Those two jobs were less than ideal because smoking at desks was allowed and because of his previous illness, it was very hard on him.

In June of 1985 Ronnie and I bought a small secretarial service in downtown Minneapolis. It was fun but we did get some unique customers. We continued with the business until August 1998 and then moved the business to the basement of my house. Later, Ronnie retired and I continued the business, which I am still doing only now there are three regular customers.

That gives a general background of Ronnie so now on to my background. I was born in St. Paul, Minnesota, on October 1, 1946. We lived in an apartment right across the street from the back of Midway Hospital where I was born. In September of 1948 we moved to a new house my folks bought in Highland Park, a newer area of St. Paul. In fact, there was a field across the street and it was not unusual to see pheasants there. In the early 50s an elementary school was built there that went up to third grade. It was completed when I was in the middle of the first grade so was transferred to that school. By the time we finished third grade an addition had been added to the school going up to the sixth grade. Those were the best years of school for me.

By the time we finished grade school, Highland Junior High School had been built two blocks away so I went there from 7th grade through 9th grade. There was a choice of two St. Paul High Schools to go to, Central or Monroe. For some reason my parents thought I would be better off going to U High which was part of the University of Minnesota. It was considered kind of a laboratory school for teachers who were working on advanced degrees and they could only stay there for seven years. It was on the U's Minneapolis campus so it meant taking a school bus.

Looking back it would have been better to go to either Central or Monroe and if I had known Ronnie graduated from Monroe, I might have gone there. The students at U High were of a different background than I was. The son of the mayor of Minneapolis went there, the State Treasurer's kids were there as was a grandson of Franklin Roosevelt. I do not look back fondly on the high school years except for one thing. I belonged to the Spanish Club and in 1963 they had a two week trip to Mexico which I went on. That was fun and a good experience.

A few months before high school graduation in 1964, I started working part time at Midway Hospital in the admitting department and also the switchboard. Working on the switchboard was fun. It was the old fashion cord board. We answered incoming calls, calls from within the hospital, paged doctors and others plus paged emergencies which then were called "Dr. Blue." Midway Hospital was where the team physician for the Minnesota Vikings practiced so when the football players had surgery it was at Midway and we admitted them. The most notable one I remember, but didn't admit myself, was Fran Tarkington.

Following high school graduation, I started at the University of Minnesota which wasn't too big of an adjustment having gone to high school there. Eventually I got a two year degree with some credits beyond but my heart really wasn't in it. Then I started a Medical Secretary program at Minnesota School of Business in downtown Minneapolis. I worked at Midway until the fall of 1970 when I got a job as a medical secretary for one of the doctors who was on the staff at Midway. Stayed at that job for about nine months, which was about nine months too long. After that, I got a job as a medical secretary at an orthopedic clinic where I worked for almost 15 years. It was then Ronnie and I bought our business.

This is our general backgrounds. Now on to our 60 years knowing each other and our 50 years together.

Meeting someone is the beginning of a relationship which you do not know where it will go or lead you to. The meeting of someone involves hopes and expectations of both people and the future. Best not to except too much when first meeting until you get to know each other but you can always hope.

In May or June of 1956 my life changed. My girlfriend, Mary Lynn, and I would go to the neighborhood grocery store in St. Paul owned by a woman named Connie, we always said we were going to "Connie's", for popsicles, candy and whatever else we wanted. One day Mary Lynn called me all excited. She had been to Connie's to get something for her mother and "there was the cutest boy" at the store. I made a beeline for her house, we went up to the store and she sure was right.

His name was Ron but we called him Ronnie. He was older than we were, although we didn't know how much older, but we didn't care. He was gorgeous, looked like he could easily be a movie star, in fact, I always thought he resembled Rock Hudson and later on told him. Over the summer vacation we made our trips to the store to not only see Ronnie but to talk to him. Mary Lynn and I were 10 years old then but I fell in love with him, of course, it was the love of a young girl. At times I went to the store on my own for something and was thrilled to talk with him.

As the years went on, we continued to go to see Ronnie and by the time we were in ninth grade Mary Lynn moved to Edina, a suburb of Minneapolis, but I continued go to see and talk with him. Later on I got my driver's permit and eventually a driver's license. The first place I drove on my own was to the store to tell Ronnie. By then I was 16 or 17.

Ronnie's father bought the store and Ronnie would work there every night. He was going to Macalester College at the time so he had to try to do some studying while working at the store. Customers would come in and make snide remarks like "still going to school" but that didn't stop him. At the time he was working toward a degree in education.

As a young girl and even into the early teen years, I would daydream about Ronnie, try to imagine what it would be like to go out with him but knowing that wouldn't happen. Or would it? In early August of 1965 I was at the store talking with Ronnie when suddenly he said "would you like to go out sometime?" Stunned, the first thing that came out of my mouth was "When?" Couldn't believe I said that. It was early in the week, he asked if Friday, August 6, would be okay. Of course it was! As I remember, it has been so many years, he said he would pick me up around 6:30 PM. Then the big question and decisions – what would I wear. It was quite a week up until Friday but probably the most exciting week of my life up until then.

Friday came and Ronnie pulled up in front of the house. I watched as he walked up to the house and couldn't believe how gorgeous he looked. He was dressed in different shades of blue, blue slacks, sport coat, shirt, and tie. He was tan, his hair was a goldish blond. I wore a blue dress so you might say we were color coordinated. He came in, talked to my folks and then we left. We were going to the Guthrie Theater in Minneapolis to see "Richard III." He parked the car and we started walking to the theater. We had to cross Hennepin Avenue which is a busy street. I was wearing high heels, was so excited and nervous I thought I probably would fall right in the middle of the street, but luckily it didn't happen.

The play was very good although I have to admit that during most of it all I could think about was being on a date with Ronnie. After the play was over, we went to a café in a downtown hotel to have something to eat. It was such a wonderful night, better than I could have ever dreamt.

That summer we went out four more times. Once more time to the Guthrie Theater to see "The Cherry Orchard." Other times we went to movies. We always went somewhere after to have something to eat.

Years later Ronnie told me that before he asked me out he asked his father if he thought it would be alright to date me being the difference in our ages. His dad told him it would fine so I have his father to thank for our beginning to go out.

After our fifth date, for some reason, we didn't go out any more that year. I would go up to the store but probably not as often as before. In the summer of 1966 things changed. We started going out again and this time it continued.

Chapter 2
Getting to Know Each Other

A t this point, the old song "Getting to Know You" is rather appropriate. Hopefully you meet someone who ends up being a person you would like to continue a relationship with. But you have to realize there is more to the relationship than just having a good time. Stop to consider if the two of you are compatible, as well as realize there is an element of give and take on the part of both of you. If these elements and true for both of you, then you have a good chance.

So many years have passed since our relationship started that remembering exactly what happened, how some things happened, and in what order they occurred is difficult, but then that probably isn't too important. What is important is what drew us together and what kept us together.

As far as I was concerned, what we did didn't really matter so long as it was together. By this time, I was 20 years old, going to the University of Minnesota and working part time at Midway Hospital in the Admitting Office and on the switchboard. Ronnie was teaching at Mechanic Arts High School and had the summers off, although he continued working in the evenings at his father's store. During the summer of 1966, we did a lot of outdoor activities such as walking, biking and swimming. Exercise was a big part of his life; as it was very important to him, I had to decide if I would make it a part of my life with him. The answer was a definite "yes" even though I was not a typical athletic type.

On my days off from the hospital, we would go to Lake Calhoun or to Excelsior on Lake Minnetonka to go swimming. He had a 1965 Corvette convertible that we used a number of times. That car was his pride and joy, so it was driven with care and caution, but riding in it with the top down and the sun shining on us was fun. When he drove the Corvette, he was like a kid again – not that drove fast or recklessly but that he got so much joy out of it. He would tell me how to shift, and as silly as it sounds, it was a big deal at that time. Our first picnic was at Lake Calhoun on July 18, 1967. I only remember the date because it was written in a photo album by a picture taken that day. That was the first of a great many picnics to come through the years.

We went to Excelsior a number of times starting in July 1968. I did not know how to swim, but he was a good swimmer. He taught me how to swim. After finally getting the hang of it and finally being able to swim as long as my feet would touch the bottom of the lake when I stopped, he taught me how to dive. We would get to waist-high water, he would bend his knee, which I would stand on and jump or dive, into the water. It may sound kind of corny, but it sure was fun. There was a stand there that two older women ran. We would get a large glass of milk with ice cubes, another simple pleasure both of us enjoyed.

When summer ended, Ronnie went back to teaching. On my days off, I would get a card or write a note, drive to the school parking lot, and place it on his windshield as a surprise when he came out after school. After he passed away, when I was going through things in his folks' house which he still owned, I found the cards and notes. You don't know what it meant to find that he kept them all those years.

In the evenings, Ronnie would read, late into the early hours. He loved to read and had enough books to make a small library. He had a wide variety of books from religion to philosophy to poetry which he loved plus many others. This is a point where we were very different. I am not a reader. He loved to share what he had been reading. We would talk on the phone every night at about 10 p.m. and could go on for an hour or even up to two hours. Sharing his love of reading and what he got from it was another important part of our relationship.

While Ronnie was home reading, I was home sewing. Granted, he didn't get excited about sewing, but he did reap the benefits of it. I made him many shirts, a couple of pairs of slacks, shirt jackets when they were popular, and even swimming trunks. One year I made us matching swimming outfits.

Both of us liked music, probably he more than me, but his enthusiasm was contagious. He was brought up with music on the radio, records and singing with family. He liked the old standards sung by Tony Bennett, Perry Como, Bing Crosby, Doris Day and many other popular singers. In the 1960s, there was a young singer by the name of John Gary who had a television show that would fill in during the summer. It turned out both of us liked him. Some years later, we found out that John Gary was going to be performing at Diamond Jim's, a dinner theater in the St. Paul area, so we went. That was the first of a number of times we saw him at

Diamond Jim's. We met him after the shows and would talk with him. One time when we were there it was in the winter, the weather was less than ideal. There was a rather small audience for the first show. When the show was over, everyone was invited to stay for the second show, which we did. One of the times when we were there, Ronnie took a picture of me with John. Later, John started appearing at the Carlton Celebrity Room Backstage in Bloomington, a suburb of Minneapolis. Again, we would enjoy his shows and talking with him.

When Ronnie would finish in the evening at the store, we would go for a walk and then come to my house for a late night snack and watch TV. We especially liked watching movies, in particular old movies from the 1940s through the 1970s. A few of our favorites are "An Affair to Remember," "It Happened One Night," and "Love is a Many Splendored Thing." Of course, he liked military-themed movies, especially involving Marines. When VCRs took hold, if there was a good movie on TV, I would record it so we could watch it later. We also went to many, many movies. Ronnie went through phases where he liked a particular actor. There was the Clint Eastwood period, a Charles Bronson era, and a few others so we would see all their current movies. Many weeks, we saw two or three movies. Being a rather sentimental person, I would keep the ticket stubs, cut out the ad in the paper for the movie, and staple both on a half-sheet of paper to keep. I still have quite a pile of papers, but it is fun to look back and see some of the good movies we saw and some that were less than good.

Okay, you discovered some of each others likes and dislikes, now comes the give and take of a relationship.

Sometimes it may be hard, but if you can share what each of you like and do not like, you have a good foundation for a relationship. Maybe one of the keys of dealing with each other's likes and dislikes is being flexible; after all, there is no black and white, and who knows – maybe after a while you might change your ideas.

Sometimes it is hard to do something the other person likes when you are not all that interested in it. With us there were the office parties or weddings that one of us was invited to and the other attended. He was not all that big on going to events where he did not know people very well, such as office parties for where I worked. They always had parties, such as at Christmas, at a nice restaurant or country club, but it was more the idea of being in a crowd of people he did not know.

He had the same feeling about weddings. For one wedding we went to, there was just one couple there that he knew. If I remember right it was someone that came in his dad's store, so that helped a little. I went to several of his relatives weddings, which at first was a little awkward being that I was rather quiet and reserved or maybe just plain shy at that time, but it turned out to be nice just being together.

When Ronnie got in a bookstore, he could spends hours looking at books. Long times spent in a bookstore was not that inviting to me. While he would be looking at books, I would wander around looking at some that may have been of more interest to me but always wound up back where he was hoping he was about ready to leave. I had to realize and accept this was a big part of him and just adjust to it.

Another part of give and take is expressing what you want. What you want to do or not do, maybe when you want a little time alone as well as when you want time together. What was important to me was our having time for us to be together but to be together alone, just the two of us. Fortunately, this was important to him too. Whether we were going somewhere together or just being at home, watching a movie on TV and having something to eat, it meant a lot to us. Maybe you could say that fortunately we were not big on being in crowds, so our alone time together was very important to us.

When Ronnie was in college, he wanted to write a journal but never got to it. In 1999, he decided he would finally write his journal. Using lined paper like you would use in school his journal began. He started on August 17, his birthday, and wrote an entry every day until his birthday in 2000, some 848 pages later. He would begin with a "Thought for the day" and then go on to a summary of the day. He would write about thoughts of the past, thoughts that meant a lot to him such as poetry, writers he admired or various books he read through the years. He would end the entry with a prayer he wrote which usually summarized the day and/or his feelings for the day. Each entry ended with "Nulla dies sine lacryma!"

Excerpts from his first entry began:

August 17, 1999 ~ I am starting today a desire which began in college, i.e., a journal of thoughts and events for my memory bank, which from a security standpoint can never be pilfered, leaving me destitute and mentally poverty ridden. So, forty some years later I begin.

Yes, my day passed as I know summer will soon pass and close its door. It seems to follow quickly on the heels of my birthday. I dislike the feeling aroused this time of year, says farewell to another summer. Thoreau is right, "Perhaps what most moves us in winter is some reminiscence of far-off summer. For we are hunters pursuing the summer on snow-shoes and skates, all winter long. There is really but one season in our hearts."

Thank you, God, for the day and all the passed days of my life. My birthdays have been abundant in offerings, gifts and attention, and perhaps at times ungraciously received, and for this I am sorry. Thank you for the gifts of parents and their families. Thank you for the gift of life.

Nulla dies sine lacryma!

And then there is this entry:

Oct. 1, 1999 – (Friday) Happy Birthday, Ann! Ann's birthday, fifty-third, was dimmed somewhat by the weather – damp, dreary, and dreary with rain in the late afternoon and evening.

It seems impossible to me that Ann has lived fifty-three years of real time knowing me. The years would appear almost imaginary speeding through the years to this moment. Much has happened to her in the past four years, beginning with her mother's physical and mental breakdown and finally death, which was followed on the heels by her father's unsettled condition, physically and mentally. But Ann has stood tall throughout all of this and has grown in the face of these bitter experiences, earning for her respect. She is a fine girl.

Thy blessings, O Lord, on the souls of the following I entreat: my parents, my grandparents, their forebearers, their descendants, and any soul who has touched my life with love sincere. I have steadfast faith in the belief of Thy mercy and Thy forgiveness of human frailties O God. Amen.

Nulla dies sine lacryma!

Many nights when we were on the telephone he would read his entry for the day, which was special, his sharing his personal thoughts with me. Now that he is gone, this journal means much more; it keeps him alive and close. On his birthday in 2017, I started reading his journal. I go downstairs to his "library" and read the day's entry. These are very special times.

Chapter 3
Honesty and Trust:
Working Lives

After meeting, dating and getting to know each other, there are several elements that will determine whether the relationship will continue and flourish or whether it will crumble and end. Probably two of the most important are honesty and trust. Without honesty and trust doom is on the horizon whether it is in your working lives, social lives or daily lives. There will probably be times when something is not fully disclosed but when it is something that is not significant to a relationship. It may be inconsequential. Just don't let it get out of control.

Through the years, Ronnie told me about some of his previous relationships. The one common element in the ones that ended on a less than cordial note was dishonesty. If he found out someone lied to him, they cut their own throat. It sometimes can be hard confessing to something, but in the end you will be the winner.

Over the years, Ronnie had a variety of different jobs from full-time teaching to part-time jobs working for the Veterans Administration and Post Office. When teaching, he dealt with students who could be less than honest. He dealt with them fairly and always wanted to help them improve themselves. There were times when he would be assertive with a student, but it always ended with them being friends. They couldn't have wanted a better teacher or friend.

When he was teaching, there was also his working relationship with the staff. For the most part, that was no issue. He was a very good-looking man and dressed well for his job. There were a few women who liked him and showed some interest, and not all of them were single. He was honest with me about what happened at school. He showed no interest in them other than as co-workers, nothing beyond that. He was friendly and personable, which can be attractive to other women, but I knew it went no farther than that. He would go out for a drink once in a while after school, but it was always with other men teachers. One teacher, who was married, quite often would get into conversations with him. He reminded her she was married, but it didn't seem to matter to her, although it definitely did to him. Ronnie was a very honest person, at times painfully so, so I would have known, or at least suspected, if there was any interest in a woman at school.

There were times both of us would have to work a little later than usual. He would stay for staff meetings or some type of school activity, which I understood. Many times I worked later because of the doctor being behind schedule; that was after his dad's store was out of business, so he was home. Because we both trusted each other, there didn't seem to be any issues. We both had to realize we had to talk with coworkers of the opposite sex, but we also realized how far conversations should go.

Both of us experienced situations at our jobs that were up-setting or stressful, but we knew we could talk to each other about them. For example, when Ronnie was working for the VA, the supervisor was a woman who appeared to almost re-sent some of the men working under her. She was not helpful when he had questions, would go over answers to questions quickly, and that was that. He would be so upset by these instances, and we would talk about. Finally, he decided the best thing was to see about transferring to another section, which he did, and I fully supported this decision.

When I was working at Children's Hospital, there was a sit-uation where a co-worker lied about something I said. There was transcription I had been doing that was eventually given to another woman in a department that worked along with ours. This was fine. When this other woman was quitting, she told me they probably would ask if I would take back the work I had done previously and that would have been fine with me. Time went on and no one said anything about my doing the work. When I started working at the hospital, this co-worker would say off and on how glad she was that I was there because she didn't like doing transcription and I would rather do that than scheduling. After some time, I couldn't figure out why she was going to be doing it when she had said over and over again she didn't like to. Eventually I talked to the department manager, and it came out that my coworker said that I made the statement I didn't want to do the work again, which was completely untrue since I was anticipating being asked to. Ronnie knew how upset I was, and we talked about it very often. I finally thought about looking for a different job since working with someone who lied about me would be less than ideal. In fact, I had an interview for another job. But then I realized there was maybe two years left before I could retire having put in 10 years, and why should I throw that time away, so I decided to stay. Things were never the same between the other woman and myself. I later realized I should have handled the situation in a different way, but I just bided my time until retirement. The one redeeming factor was that she was not particularly well thought of by other people in the department. Most importantly, Ronnie supported me throughout, which meant the world to me.

When we bought our business, times were challenging as far as the work and the customers; of the latter, we did get some strange ones. Ronnie's father passed away not long after taking on our business, which resulted in my working more alone due in a large part because his mother really didn't want him alone with me at work every day. Eventually he worked one day a week. I didn't say much about the situation to him because he had enough to deal with losing his father and the way his mother was acting.

About two years after working our business, I had to have surgery, which meant Ronnie had to take over. He did the best he could and would call me often with questions. After I got back to work, our business was starting to decline. In some ways, we didn't mind because whether we were busy or not, it gave us the chance to be alone together.

Eventually, we decided to close the office downtown and moved it to my house. Part of our business was an answering service that had to be discontinued, but some of the work for other regular customers continued by their faxing or mailing work or tapes for transcription. Ronnie more or less retired from the job, and I had to get a part-time job to supplement income. At the time, my folks were experiencing issues with their health and aging, so I could not take a full-time job. We didn't set the world on fire with our business nor did we become wealthy, but we enjoyed our time together.

Our jobs did not involve some of the pitfalls found in other work situations. Neither of us had to do any traveling for our work. Ronnie didn't have to work overtime. I did work overtime the days patients were seen in the clinic and we had to stay until all patients had been seen but that involved maybe an hour or hour and a half. By that time I was so ready to leave there were no thoughts of anything else.

Through the years, the strength of our relationship came down to how honest we were with each other and how much we trusted each other. If you want your relationship to succeed, be sure that you are honest with each other right from the beginning because once dishonesty is discovered it can be the start of a loss of trust between two people. In fact, all of what is described above happened before we were married, so it was a very good test of our relationship.

Chapter 4
Faithfulness to Each Other: Influences

F aithfulness to each other is very important. How you can be faithful to each other despite outside influences such as family – particularly parents – and friends or just hearing stories that you hear over and over can be difficult. In our relationship, the outside influences were parents and to a lesser extent friends, particularly people I worked with. If the relationship is important, you have to be patient, but your patience will be well worth it.

One of the people in our lives who required a lot of patience was Ronnie's mother, Mary. From the time he was a very small child, his mother engrained in him deep devotion to her. It was fine until after his father passed way, and then she went all out to break us up, to the point that it brought on Ronnie's heart attack. For some reason, she had the idea the two of us were going to take off and leave her alone. After this continued for some time, he made clear to her that we were not going to part, so she had to adjust to it.

One day I went over to their house. The basement steps were straight ahead of the back door, and both of them were downstairs. As I headed down the steps, his mother stood at the bottom. I got about halfway down the steps, when out of the blue she said, "You can have him when I'm through with him." I couldn't believe what I heard. Ronnie heard her but asked me what she said, probably not believing his ears. I repeated it. I do not remember what he said, but he was not happy. My first thought was *By the time you are through with him, there won't be anything left of him.*

She remained on the warpath trying to come between us for a long time. It affected Ronnie to the point that in September 1986 he had a heart attack. Six weeks later, he underwent a triple bypass. During this time, I continued working at our business in downtown Minneapolis. Every morning my dad would drive Mary to the hospital as she never learned to drive. She would be there until evening when I came. I would be by the foot of the bed, as we watched "Wheel of Fortune." If Ronnie and I were alone, watching TV wouldn't have been top on the list. When it was time to go, we would leave together, and I drove her home, which many times was a very quiet ride. This tension and stress didn't make his recovery easy. Several times after taking her home, I went back to the hospital to spend time alone with him. One evening when I got there, his mother was sitting in a chair with her coat on. Ronnie said to take her home. *Here she goes again*, I thought. I did take her home but then went back to the hospital. I do not remember what had happened before I got there, but it didn't help his recovery.

For a long time, I knew I wanted to marry Ronnie. After his father passed away, I understood that if we did get married his mother would end up living with us, which would never have worked out. We wouldn't have been able to be ourselves with her there. A decision was necessary: We either get married and start out on our own or I would move on. By doing this, I would run the risk of him saying no. A third option existed, though: continue our relationship as it was. That was the decision for which I opted. It was better than not being with him at all. Besides, except that we were not living together, it was almost like we were married. In my heart, we were married. In the years to come, it did prove to be the right decision.

Fortunately, my mother was not so much of a negative influence, but she felt that eventually nothing would come of our relationship, maybe because of his mother. My mother liked Ronnie, and they would talk, but her feeling was "He will never marry you." Our getting married wasn't as important as being with him, though. Besides, there were many people who were together for years that never married, particularly celebrities such as Kathryn Hepburn and Spencer Tracy or Goldie Hawn and Kurt Russell. Granted, their situations were different, but they stayed together. In some ways, we had the best of both worlds – we were together the majority of the time and we also had our time apart. Maybe that added to our longevity.

Despite his mother's quest to break us up, when she was older – she lived to be three-and-a-half months short of 103 – and her health was failing, I was there to help her. The past was not important then. For the most part, she had her wits about her but at times just didn't seem to use her head. She got so she had to use a walker, which had been Ronnie's father's. The walker did not have wheels on it, so she had to lift it with each step, which she managed well. For some reason, there were times when she would turn the walker around ending up with less than ideal consequences. One day, Ronnie and I got back to their house only to find her on the floor after turning the walker around the wrong way. Her legs were caught in the walker, so we had to untangle her and then get her up, which was not always an easy task. She was only 5'2" tall, weighing around 90 pounds, but when she fell she was dead weight.

There was more than one occasion when Ronnie called me late in the evening saying his mother had fallen and he couldn't get her up. I always went over right away to the house to help. It took both of us to get her up. Later, she was pretty much confined to bed, so I brought my mother's commode to put at its side. Eventually she needed maximum help getting on the commode, and I was there to help her, which may in turn have helped him too.

The point of telling some of the instances that occurred here is not to make me look good but to point out that despite all the grief Ronnie's mother caused, I couldn't not help her. There were many years when she was very generous and actually fun; those were before Ronnie's father died. She was a fantastic cook, and I had more delicious meals that she had made then I could ever count. Considering all that, there was no way I could turn my back on her.

Friends also can have a negative influence on your relationship. Ronnie's friends didn't seem to have any problem with our being together, but mine seemed to. The one thing my friends and co-workers would ask was his age. They were younger than me, so being with someone 17 years older may have seemed strange to them to say the least. My answer would be "he is a little older than I am" never telling them his actual age. I felt that it was really none of their business. It didn't bother me, so it shouldn't bother them.

Another effect of friends' influences can be from their asking "Aren't you married yet?" in Ronnie's case and "When are you getting married?" in my case. Maybe they just couldn't stand seeing two people being happy but not married, or, who knows, maybe in some way they were jealous. More than one person asked Ronnie if he was married, and when he said no, they didn't seem to understand it. One thing I discovered is that you cannot live your life according to what other people think or feel; it just won't work. How you, as a couple, live your lives is really none of their business.

It boils down to what is more important – what other people think or how you want to live your life. Maybe some people couldn't stand to see us so happy because they were married but unhappy. You never know. So, if you are happy with your lives as a couple, live it, enjoy it, cherish it, and don't worry about what other people think.

Sometimes boredom will creep into a relationship, but you can't allow that to destroy your faithfulness to one another. Instead, you must remain patient. For example, you'll soon hear stories that you have heard more than once. I realized that it didn't matter how many times I heard the story in the past, what mattered was that he wanted to share them with me. Besides, he probably heard the same thing from me more than once. If you hear stories over and over, you may realize in the future how important they become. They are part of your loved one that will stay with you always.

In fact, the day will come when you will look back upon those stories with fondness. One such story for me was just before Christmas the woman that Ronnie was going with suggested that he be Santa and she would be Mrs. Claus and they would go to homes delivering presents to the children.

He liked the idea, so she put an ad in the newspaper. The family would put gifts outside of the house, Ronnie and his girlfriend would show up at a designated time, they would pick up the gifts outside, and bring them in for the kids. The majority of the homes they went to were in poor sections of the city. Ronnie felt empathy for the children and the families, but when he saw the looks on the kids' faces and heard the excitement in their voices, he was so happy he played Santa. Ronnie said it made his Christmas mean much more that year.

Another story I heard a few times was when he was at a driving range hitting golf balls. As with all sports, he was very good at golf. There was a woman at the driving range trying to hit balls, and when she saw Ronnie, her way of striking up a conversation was to ask for his help. She told him how good he was at hitting the golf balls and asked what was she doing wrong. After a while, she brought up about going out sometime. A date was arranged. Ronnie picked her up and in their conversation in the car he asked her what kind of work she did. She said she was a stockbroker. Stocks was all she talked about all evening. He could hardly wait to get her home. Needless to say, that was their one and only date.

In the early years of our dating, Ronnie mentioned a number of women he had gone out with, but it usually ended up with the woman lying to him, and that was the end. According to Ronnie, the women were good looking, some talented, or some with good jobs. After a while, I started to get kind of jealous. But one day I woke up realizing there was nothing to be jealous of since I was the one with him then. After that, hearing about previous women didn't matter.

Chapter 5
Growth of Relationship

There are two factors that help the growth of a relationship. One is to enjoy and cherish your time together during the good times. The other is to learn and grow from the hard times. Hopefully there will be many years of good times but you have to know there will be hard times so be prepared.

Over the 50 years we were together we had more good times than I could ever count. From the beginning we enjoyed our summers outdoors. We started by going to nearby lakes but a few years into our relationship we started to take trips to some of the nearby small towns, usually within a 50 mile radius or less. We loved to go to Stillwater which had a very early start in Minnesota, called "The Birthplace of Minnesota." The St. Croix River runs along the eastern border of Stillwater. We used to go to a park by the river for picnics. There were several restaurants we enjoyed plus wonderful stores for shopping.

Another favorite place of ours was Northfield, Minnesota. Northfield is the home of Carlton College, St. Olaf College and the infamous Jesse James bank robbery. We found a place on the campus of Carlton College we enjoyed very much for our picnics. Sometimes we would bring a small grill to cook corn on the cob. Ronnie had a cotton blanket that we would spread on the ground. There were several times we were at Carlton when it got chilly so we just wrapped the blanket around us to keep nice and warm. Most of the time after we finished eating, we drove to the small downtown area. There were a number of small shops with very nice clothes that you wouldn't find in the bigger stores in the Twin Cities. I bought many clothes there, some of which I still have only by now many of them do not fit. Time has a way of doing that.

Northfield is well known for their Jesse James Days in the fall. The town re-enacted the bank robbery which was fun. There were tents with events going on including bingo. We played bingo several times with Ronnie winning $16 once. They also had food stands with fair type foods. We went to Northfield for this event a number of times.

South of Northfield is Faribault, home of the Faribault Woolen Mills. We started going to Faribault regularly too. Sometimes we had picnics or would eat at a restaurant called the Lavender Inn. Their food was wonderful. Attached to the restaurant was a gift shop. We loved wandering around there to see what they had. They had a stuffed warthog which was fun to see. They had a very nice roll top desk that Ronnie liked and eventually bought. It was not the typical size desk, smaller, more conducive to his needs. Unfortunately some years back the Lavender Inn was sold and torn down but we had our memories.

We had numerous one day trips in the Twin Cities area but nothing could compare to our trips to Chicago. Quite often my dad would get a Chicago Sunday paper. Once I was looking through the paper and found an ad for a play that was going to be at one of the theaters. The play was *Twentieth Century*

THE TWO OF US ARE ONE   41

Limited starring Rock Hudson. Rock Hudson was my favorite actor so that got my interest. This was in August of 1979 and since Ronnie's birthday was August 17, I asked him if he would like to go to Chicago to see the play for his birthday. Much to my surprise and pleasure, he said yes. I mentioned flying since it only takes an hour or less but he didn't want to fly so we took the Amtrak train.

On a Friday evening about 11:00 pm the train pulled out of the St. Paul station headed for Chicago with the two of us. We had one compartment but had to pay for two tickets which was fine. This was our first real adventure away from home. We managed to get a little sleep that night before the train pulled into Union Station in Chicago around 7:00 am. The play wasn't until the afternoon. What were we going to do until then? I remembered the name of the Congress Hotel on Michigan Avenue so we took a cab there to eat breakfast. By the time we finished eating and sat in the lobby for a while it was time for the businesses and stores to open, off we headed walking down Michigan Avenue. By noon we went back to the Congress Hotel, decided to get a room then we could have a place to put the goodies we bought and as a place to rest after the play until leaving for the 11:00 pm train. After getting settled, we got a cab and headed for the Arie Crown Theater. This was the first of three plays we saw at the Arie Crown Theater. The other two were *Camelot* starring Richard Burton and *My Fair Lady starring Rex Harrison.*

The play wasn't the best and at times Rock Hudson seemed rather awkward but I was seeing Rock Hudson in person with Ronnie, what could have been better? After the play was over, we walked to a nearby restaurant for something to eat, both of us were hungry. From there we took a cab to the Congress hotel. About 10:30 pm we took a cab to the train station to head home. Although we were dead tired by the time we got home Sunday morning, it was well worth it because it was a fabulous day.

This was the first of a number of trips to Chicago. The first four we took the Amtrak train. We would get a room at the Congress Hotel where we could put our purchases while we would go to eat. One of the restaurants we went to was Berghoff which specializes in German cuisine. I had been there years before with my parents and it seemed the same as it was the first time there. They have the most delicious food and if I remember correctly, they make their own beer and ginger ale. After eating, we headed back to the hotel to relax until time to head for the train.

One of the times we took the train we had fallen asleep on the way to Chicago and woke up when we were almost at the station. Did we ever get ready fast. Another time when we were leaving to go home, we took a cab to the station. The driver let us out about a block or more away from the station so we had to walk to the station at about 10:30 pm. Needless to say, we were not happy.

A few years later I saw an ad that John Gary was going to be performing at Pheasant Run Resort in St. Charles, Illinois, a suburb of Chicago, in their dinner theater. We decided to go to see him but since the train didn't stop in St. Charles we drove. We left on a Friday morning and came back on Sunday. Late Saturday morning we drove into Chicago for our usual shopping and walking along Michigan Avenue. On one of the previous trips I saw a Snoopy cookie jar in a store and was sorry later I didn't get it since I like Snoopy. During one of our subsequent trips we tried to remember where we saw the cookie jar. We started canvassing the stores we usually go to. Bingo, we finally found it. Naturally I bought it. It was in a good size box and we carried that around downtown Chicago but it was worth it.

We sat at a table with another couple from Chicago for the evening show. The husband was a Chicago policeman. When we talked about driving into Chicago earlier in the day, he asked what way we went. When we said we drove in on North Avenue, both he and his wife said it was the worst way we could have gone. On subsequent trips, we found less risky routes to take. The show was very good as usual and afterwards we stopped to talk with John and his wife. As usual, we bought either a record or cassette. The next day we headed home.

Our trips to Chicago brought us even closer together being able to spend the time away from home alone. All our adventures either near home, out of town or in Chicago were memories we cherished and through the following years talked about them often.

As nice as the good times were, there were also hard times. The worst time was when Ronnie had his heart attack in September of 1986. His mother wanted to call an ambulance but he wanted to wait until I got to the house. When I did get there, he wanted to ride in the car to the hospital. That was the scariest ride of my life. He was writhing in pain. When he got in the Emergency Room at Midway Hospital, the doctor said there was a medication they could give him to try to dissolve the blood clot but he wasn't sure it would work. Thank God it did! That didn't mean everything was fine. The doctors did find that the heart attack caused some damage to heart because of the delay in getting to the hospital but the damage was in the back of the heart which they said was better than if the damage was in the front of the heart. He was in the hospital at least a week when he had to be transferred to United Hospital for an angiogram as they did not do cardiac angiograms at Midway Hospital. He was able to go to United in the car so I drove the three of us. The angiogram showed three clogged arteries which meant he was a candidate for a triple bypass. He was discharged to go home and triple bypass surgery was scheduled for October 22, 1986. The time before the surgery was to give him time to gain strength prior to the surgery.

Ronnie was readmitted to United Hospital on October 21 for surgery the following day. When he was being taken to surgery, his mother and I went with to the preop area to be with him before going into surgery. When they were going to take him to surgery, I gave him a kiss and told him I love him. I cannot remember exactly how long the surgery lasted but it seemed like forever. Following surgery he was in the Cardiac Intensive Care Unit for three days. Ronnie's internist was in visiting him when he made the comment that he had a patient who lived 20 years after bypass surgery. I thought it was something that should not have been said since it could be taken as not encouraging. Ronnie lived just short of 30 years after the surgery.

His recovery was probably a little slower than hoped for but he did progress well except for the development of arrhythmia, irregular heart rhythm. He was having some cardiac rehabilitation in the form of physical therapy. When there to visit him, he was able to get up and walk around the unit he was in which was encouraging. He was discharged from the hospital on November 3. Since I had to be at our office, my father brought his mother to the hospital, later drove Ronnie and his mother home. Snow started falling before they left the hospital.

After being home just a few days, he decided he would start walking outside. Each day he would walk a little further. When the walking was going well, he started to jog. He would go a short distance jogging, walk and then jog again. He did this despite the snow on the ground. After he had been doing this for several days, he noticed improvement.

Ronnie worked hard at rehabilitating himself on his own at home. Eventually he started using his hand weights. He also got an exercise bicycle which he kept in the attic. He used the bike everyday no matter how cold or hot it was in the attic. In fact, he wore out two exercise bikes. He also got a Nordic Track ski type exerciser which he used religiously every day for 30 to 45 minutes a day. Ronnie did amazing with his recovery but when he decided to do something, he stuck to his plan.

Everything went well for Ronnie after his surgery. In March of 1987 I developed some medical problems which resulted in having a hysterectomy on April 1. I recommend *not* having surgery on April 1 if at all possible. The surgeon anticipated there could be problems later in the day because there were so many blood vessels involved when she did the surgery and significant blood replacement because of the loss. Sure enough, later that afternoon the surgeon came in and told me they were going to do more surgery in the evening. I called Ronnie to tell him and asked the nurse to call my parents. Apparently because my blood pressure was low from blood loss, I didn't get too upset about the second surgery.

After the surgery was over, I woke up in the recovery room. All I remember was seeing my folks, Mary and Ronnie at the foot of the bed. I remember Ronnie squeezing my big toe. The next thing I knew I woke up in the middle of the night but not in a regular room, I was in Intensive Care. There was a man standing next to the bed who introduced himself as my nurse. After that type of surgery, you rather hope for a female nurse but he was very nice. The following day I was moved to a regular room, hooked up to all kinds of tubes including a nasogastric tube, I couldn't eat anything, just suck on ice chips. After a day or two, I was able to get up and walk in the hall. When Ronnie was there, we would walk the halls together once everything was disconnected. After about a week, I was discharged home but could not go back to work for six weeks. A few days later I began going outside to walk, similar to what Ronnie did but without the jogging. That year we had beautiful weather in April which made it easier to get outside.

Things went well for both of us until about 2012 or 2013, can't remember anymore, when I was lying in bed, ran my hand down my extended left arm. Just above the elbow I felt something like a hard ball. I kept checking it, told Ronnie about it and eventually told Dr. Thompson about it. Dr. Thompson was one of the orthopedic surgeons at the clinic where I had worked for almost 15 years before we bought our business. Dr. Thompson had retired from active practice but was doing what is called independent medical evaluations. Through a chance meeting at a funeral, Dr. Thompson asked if I would do his office work and schedule appointments which I could do at home along with the other business work. That turned out to be a wonderful addition to the business. Dr. Thompson checked the bump in the arm and recommended I see an orthopedic surgeon. He recommended a woman he knew who I did see. Because the bump could be either benign or malignant, surgery was recommended. The surgery was carried out on an outpatient basis. It was a benign Schwannoma. How's that for a word!

Ronnie stayed with me for two nights after getting home then went back to his house as he didn't like leaving it empty for too long. After the second day, the temperature got into the 90s with high humidity and his house did not have air conditioning so I got him to come back to stay with me. Except for going over to his house off and on during the day, we stayed together at my house from then on. So something good did come out of having to have surgery.

Other events that we went through together and ended up bringing us closer was losing our parents. His father passed away in June of 1985, my mother January 1999, my father November 2000 and his mother December 24, 2011. We were there for each all four times. Ronnie's mother passed away at home. When he thought there was something wrong with her, he called me. After I got to the house, we called 911. The paramedics confirmed that she was gone. The funeral home came to get her and it turned out one of the men used to be at the funeral home near my house and I had made arrangements for both my parents with him. Being acquainted with him made everything a little easier.

In a relationship there will be good times and bad times like we had but how a couple reacts to the events can determine the outcome of the relationship. As mentioned in the beginning of this chapter, cherish the good times and learn from the bad times, by doing this hopefully you can be closer together as we were.

Chapter 6
Know the End Will Come

As time went on, both of us were getting older, and because Ronnie was 17 years older than me, the possibility of my being left alone would come to mind now and then. I tried not to dwell on it. Because he worked so hard at keeping himself in as good of health as possible, I told him if I had anything to do with it he would get to be at least 105.

The first major incident occurred in late March 2013. Ronnie had gotten up about 4 a.m. to go to the bathroom. I was awake, and heard a loud commotion in the bathroom. As I as ran to get there, he called my name. I anticipated finding him on the floor, which would have been preferable to what actually happened. He had taken a step backward, not realizing how close he was to the bathtub. He tripped over the tub, causing him to fall backward into the tub crossways. The back of his right shoulder hit the bar on the ceramic soap dish so hard he broke the bar off. I was trying to help him get up, but we couldn't do it, so together we managed to turn him lengthwise in the tub. That didn't work either. Finally I had to call 911. The paramedics came soon. There were two men and two women. One of the men was about 6'7" or 6'8" tall and built like a redwood tree. He and the other man got in front and behind Ronnie in the tub lifting him right up. I brought a chair in the hall, and they got him to chair to sit down. They wanted to take him to the hospital, but he wouldn't go. In retrospect, he should have gone.

While the men worked with Ronnie, one of the women was with me in the kitchen looking at the back of my left hand, which had somewhat of a deep cut from pressing against the broken edge of the broken soap dish bar. She helped clean it off and put a bandage on it. At last, after the paramedics felt Ronnie was stable enough and helped him get into bed, they left.

Naturally, Ronnie was sore and in pain for the next few days but was able to get up and walk around. I remember he was in the kitchen, wearing a tank top, when I noticed for the first time the significant deep purple bruising behind his right shoulder, under the arm, and on his back from the fall. I took a picture so he could see it.

As the days went on, his back continued in pain, but I could not get him to go to see a doctor, as he feared they would recommend surgery. I saw an ad on TV for Physicians Neck & Back Clinic (PNBC) where the treatment appeared to basically be physical therapy. After calling PNBC to get more information and finding out their treatment is non-invasive, I finally managed to get Ronnie to agree to go there with the stipulation that if he didn't like it he could quit. He was seen by a physician at the initial visit, and a program was set up for him consisting of various types of machines to strengthen the muscles. Ronnie continued for several months, and by the end of the program, he was standing up straight and was more comfortable.

Things were finally as good as could be expected, and we continued doing what we had to do and wanted to do until the following Valentine's Day. We were going to go grocery shopping but first stopped at his house. Coming out of the house, Ronnie slipped on a patch of ice, landing on his back on the sidewalk. Because of the ice, I couldn't get him up and had to get the next door neighbor to help. His back was again in significant pain, and I managed to get him to agree to go back to PNBC, which he did. He did improve but did not get as good of a result as he did the first time around. When he was up walking, he could not straighten his back, causing him to stand bent over. But Ronnie continued on the best he could as he always did having to limit some of his activity more than he did before the fall.

For a number of years, we did our grocery shopping at the Cub store in Edina even though we lived in St. Paul, about 10 miles away. We became acquainted with some of the cashiers there, which made it more fun. Some time back when we were shopping at another store, a cashier made the comment she never saw two people who had more fun grocery shopping than we did, and she was right. One day when we were in line to check out at Cub, there was a customer ahead of us, so we had to wait. While waiting, Ronnie started to sing in a very soft voice. We got up to the cashier, Laurice Sovis, who we had gotten to know, and she asked him what he was singing, so he sang for her. The next week when we were there, Laurice asked him what he was going sing. His singing in the checkout line became a routine, and not only did the employees of the store enjoy it but so did customers. One time when we were there, another cashier suggested putting a video of him singing on YouTube. My first reaction, not knowing much about YouTube, was "That's the dumbest thing I ever heard of." After thinking about the idea, though, I brought our camera and took a video of him singing at the store. The man who serviced our computer came to the house to show me how to put a video on YouTube, and in January 2014 Ronnie's first video was posted. I thought if five or ten people looked at it, it would be fun. As of this writing, there are a total of 19 videos on YouTube with a total number of views for the 19 videos of just under 11,000. Doesn't seem bad for an unknown singer!

In the early summer of 2015, the need to make future plans became apparent. We would have to do something in case either of us had to go to the hospital but could not speak or make decisions for ourselves. Probably in July I brought this thought up to Ronnie suggesting that we should get married. After explaining the idea to him, he agreed that we should get married. It wasn't the reason for getting married – we did love each other very much, so it was not going to be a marriage of just convenience. I am a member of Gloria Dei Lutheran Church in St. Paul while Ronnie was not affiliated with any particular church, so I contacted Gloria Dei. We arranged to meet with one of the ministers. We met with Javon Swanson and gave him background information about us. The date for the wedding was set for August 6, 2015. I picked August 6 since that was the date of our first date, and it was not many days away.

The plan was for a very small wedding. The neighbor next door, Nancy, said for years that when Ronnie and I got married she and her husband, Dan, would stand up for us, so they were our witnesses. I thought we should have one of his relatives and one of mine at the wedding. I asked his aunt, Margaret, and she seemed excited about it. Her son, Greg, would have to drive her to the wedding since she never learned to drive, and she was 96 years old at the time. I asked one of my cousins, Nancy, and she would bring her friend Wes. All seemed to be set until Margaret said she wouldn't be coming. Greg told her she couldn't go up the steps. Ronnie would not have been able to go up the steps either; that was why we were going to park in the driveway by the door where there would be no steps. Since Margaret would not be coming to the wedding, Nancy and Dan and Nancy and Wes would be our guests. I got a tripod for the camcorder so we could make a video of the wedding. Everything went well. On August 6, we were finally married. Following the wedding, everyone came to the house for a reception, so to speak.

Laurice worked part-time at Cub with a full-time job cooking at a daycare facility. She told me that a few years earlier one of the local television stations did a story about daycare facilities and had filmed where she worked. She got the idea of them doing a story about Ronnie singing at Cub. She sent the station an e-mail but never heard back. Another local station, KARE 11, has stories on Sunday during the 10 p.m. news titled *Boyd Huppert's Land of 10,000 Stories* featuring stories about people in Minnesota and Western Wisconsin. Laurice called Boyd, but they ended up playing telephone tag. I got the idea to send him an e-mail with the idea for the story about Ronnie singing at Cub and finally did it. One day the phone rang, and it was Boyd Huppert. He said if Cub would let them film there, he would do the story. The manager agreed to the filming. Late the afternoon of Saturday, October 17, 2015, Ronnie and I met Boyd and Bill, the photographer, at Cub. Saturday was our usual day for shopping. Since Ronnie's fall in the bathtub, he developed some early signs of dementia but wasn't too bad. Boyd called the day before the filming to ask what kind of a car we had and where we park so that he and Bill could be outside waiting for us. As I pulled into the parking spot, Ronnie announced he would wait in the car. I told him that wouldn't work. Boyd came right over to the car, I told him what Ronnie said, he went around the car, talked to him, and Ronnie got out of the car. Boyd put a microphone on Ronnie and then on me, which I never expected. We were to go in the store, do our shopping as usual with Boyd asking questions as he and Bill followed us. Laurice was inside at her register. When we finished our shopping, we went to Laurice's line, chatted with her, and Ronnie sang.

The filming went very well, Ronnie sang the Marine Corps hymn, and after finishing the filming we took pictures. We found out that Boyd had set up iPads or tablets around the store playing some of Ronnie's YouTube videos. The story aired on November 10, 2015, the day before Veterans' Day. That was the biggest thrill both of us ever had. Boyd sent us a DVD of the story, and for quite a while afterwards, Ronnie and I would watch the DVD before going to sleep. Boyd is one of the nicest people anyone could ever want to meet, which made the experience all the more special.

After the TV story, Ronnie's health declined. He showed more signs of dementia, and walking became more difficult.

As time went on, getting around was harder for Ronnie. Early in spring 2016, he was having some health issues for which I called 911, and we went to Regions Hospital Emergency Room. Ronnie was admitted for a few days then transferred to a transitional care facility for physical therapy. He did well enough that he could walk with my mother's walker and function at home. He was having some skin issues, so homecare was set up through Our Lady of Peace Hospice and Homecare consisting of nursing services and a physical therapist coming to the house. The skin issues resolved and his therapy helped considerably.

Not too long after, Ronnie ended up in Regions Hospital again, which resulted in his going back to the transitional care unit for more therapy. Unfortunately, this time the therapy did not go as well. Eventually he came home and after a short time became pretty much bedridden. I had recorded a number of old movies that we liked so he enjoyed watching them.

In early August 2016, Ronnie's health declined dramatically. He became quite sick to the point on August 8, about 5 a.m., I called 911, and we went back to Regions Hospital. He was admitted to Intensive Care. He was in Intensive Care from Monday to Wednesday when the doctors told me he should be moved to a nursing home. That was devastating to hear since I knew it meant the end was approaching. I asked about his going to Our Lady of Peace, but they did not have an available bed at that time. I asked one of the doctors if Ronnie could stay at the hospital but move to another room, as I felt the move would take too much out of him and bring about the end sooner. They agreed, and later that day he was moved to a room on the floor where he would get comfort care only. In the late afternoon, I took a quick trip home to feed the cat and close the drapes and blinds, as the plan was to stay all night at the hospital to be with Ronnie. Later the next morning, I took another quick run home to feed the cat and open the drapes and blinds so it looked like someone was home. The same routine was carried out Wednesday afternoon and Thursday morning occurred.

The morning of Friday, August 12, 2016, one of the doctors came in to talk to me. For some reason, I had the awful feeling that was going to be Ronnie's last day. I mentioned this feeling to the doctor, and he agreed. I think from late Wednesday evening through Friday, Ronnie was unconscious. His condition seemed to be the same, so I took another quick trip home, probably a little faster than before. Whenever I would come back to his room, I could always hear his heavy breathing. This time when I got back, I opened the door and listened for the heavy breathing, but there was silence. I went right over to him but could hear nothing. I pressed the call button for the nurse. When she came in to check him, she confirmed my worst fear – the love of my life was gone. I held his head in my arms kissing his precious face, which then was very cold. My suspicion was that he passed away shortly after I left to go home. I have heard that many times a person will pass away after family has left so they are not there when it happens. Knowing Ronnie, that was probably what he did even if it was unconsciously. After the tubes and machines were disconnected, I was left to be alone with him. I called Laurice and Mary Lynn, in Alaska, to let them know. After being with him for quite some time, the nurse came in. I told her I was going to leave because I could not bear to see them take him out of the room knowing where he was going. As hard as it was losing my parents, this was by far more devastating.

Reality really hit when I had to make the funeral arrangements. Earlier in the year, Ronnie and I talked about where we would be buried. We finally decided on Fort Snelling National Cemetery, a place he was entitled to because of his time in the Marine Corps, and being Ronnie's wife, I can be buried there too. My cousin Patti said she would go with to make funeral arrangements, which made it easier; we made the arrangements on Monday. I was told to bring his clothes and decided to bring what he wore when we got married. The funeral was at 11 a.m. with a lunch to follow before leaving for Fort Snelling. Ronnie had a 5" x 7" picture of me in a frame in his bedroom which, if I say so myself, was a pretty good picture. I brought that one and two pictures of the two of us together to the funeral asking the director if they could be put with him. He thought they should go under his jacket over his heart, which I agreed with, as it felt like he wasn't so alone, which comforted me.

Following the lunch, we got in the procession and left for Fort Snelling. I had never been there for a funeral, so I wasn't sure what to expect. After closing the casket at the funeral home, a flag was draped over it. When we got to Fort Snelling, we went to one of the committal shelters. The Volunteer Memorial Rifle Squad lined up across the street. One of the volunteers was at the shelter with us and explained the first firing of the 21-gun salute would sound loud. He wasn't kidding. The flag was removed from the casket, folded very precisely, and presented to me which, as nice as it was, was rather difficult to accept since it was just one more confirmation of what happened to Ronnie. After the brief service, we left the cemetery, but I was told I could come back after 3 pm. I did return the following day, and although I had the section and grave numbers, it took a little time to find Ronnie since Fort Snelling Cemetery is huge. No headstone was there then; that came a little later.

After getting home from the funeral, the reality of everything hit even more. From then on, I would be home without the love of my life, which was an unpleasant prospect. A few people said that it would get easier as time goes on, but it hasn't. If anything, it seems harder, but maybe I am making it harder.

So the work would begin. Taking care of his bank accounts, his annuity, canceling his health insurance, and all the other miscellaneous necessities to be dealt with. Those turned out to be the easy things to deal with. As mentioned earlier, Ronnie still owned his parents' home, so I was left to deal with that. I probably could have sold it as is, but that didn't seem like a good option. First I needed to find a real estate agent. As mentioned in Chapter 5, years before I worked at an orthopedic clinic where Dr. Wayne Thompson was one of the orthopedic surgeons. Dr. Thompson asked if I knew any real estate agents, and when I said no, he mentioned the son of a good friend of his. Dr. Thompson checked with his friend to see if his son would be interested in selling it; when he said yes, Dr. Thompson gave me his name, Brad Osterbauer with RE/MAX Results, and phone number. I called Brad, who wanted to take a look at the house and said he would help with selling it.

Brad and I made arrangements to meet at the house. The house was built in 1942, so it was older but in a very nice area of South Minneapolis. Minnehaha Creek is across the street from the house making it very picturesque. The Light Rail transportation was to the east of the house going from downtown Minneapolis to the airport and on to the Mall of America. Brad felt it would sell especially because of the location and the Light Rail.

The house needed some fixing up like painting the exterior. When I would pull the back door shut, chips of paint would fall to the ground, but that was not a big problem. The ceiling light fixture in the eating area of the kitchen had bruned out, so it needed replacing, plus I got new light fixtures for the bathroom as well as a new sink. All relatively minor fixes. There was some plumbing work that needed to be done, and the washing machine did not work. I decided to replace both the washer and dryer so the set matched. The single attached garage had the original wood door, and even after painting it didn't look very good. The door was replaced, and an automatic opener installed. These plus a few other minor things were done by professionals.

Don't think I got by easy. The carpet in the living room, dining room and hall had seen better days, so I got on my hands and knees removed all the carpet. The hardwood floor underneath was in good condition and looked even better after cleaning it up with Aulwood. It was a big project to do alone but got done in stages.

The next project I took on was painting the woodwork and inside doors white along with the mantel. The windows were the colonial style with wood grills, which also needed painting. Those and the doors were a real pain to do. After the windows were finished, Patti came and helped scrape paint off the glass, which was a tremendous help. The place was starting to look very nice inside and out. In fact, at one point I considered possibly selling my house and living there but then decided against it.

When the inside work was well on the way, the next overwhelming task was to go through everything in the house. Again, Patti came over several times to help go through things in the attic. This was all going on during the summer, and it was HOT up in the attic. Ronnie loved to read, and there were enough books in the house to set up a small library. There was no way I could keep all the books, so Patti and I started going through them.

Ronnie had several collections. One was guns. There was one in the linen closet outside his bedroom door in case someone broke in. I assumed it was not loaded as there was a leather strip holding the cartridges. While going through the closet in his bedroom, I found two more guns. I put the three guns in a carrying case, took them home, and brought them to a police station near my house to see if they would check to see if the guns were loaded. Luckily they were not. The officer asked if I was interested in selling them, which I was. He said there were two officers, one retired and the other still working, who bought and sold guns but sold them only to other policemen. That sounded like a good option so the guns would not get into the wrong hands of people on the street. I contacted one of the officers, and they were interested. While continuing to go through the house, I came across more guns, a total of 13. I had been with Ronnie when he bought some of them years ago when you could get them at sporting goods stores but had no idea he had that many. The officers bought all 13.

Another collection Ronnie had was coins. When his dad still had the store and the silver coins were starting to have copper in the middle, Ronnie would pull out the all silver coins and save them. I got the name of a reputable coin and collectible store. Over a period of 17 to 18 weeks, sometimes twice a week, I would take bags of coins to them. Like with the guns, I had no idea of how extensive the coin collection was or how profitable. I even found a few gold fillings from teeth that they bought.

Ronnie had a 1980 Buick Regal that had not been driven for a while and was in need of some repair. With this, too, I got lucky and sold it as well as his motorcycle since there was no way I was going to learn to drive it. The other gem he had was the 1965 Corvette convertible. He had not driven the car for more than 30 years, although periodically he would talk about getting it running again. After having a few people look at it to buy, I decided to keep it. I got the name of business that specialized in classic cars and had worked on many Corvettes. After talking with them, I had the car brought to their shop, which was the nicest and cleanest auto repair facility I have ever seen. Turned out they really didn't have to do a lot of work – just replace hoses, a water pump, and tires. When it was ready, the owner of the shop brought the car to a secure, heated storage facility. When they took the car out of the trailer, it looked like it just came from the factory. They said they had never worked on a Corvette like this one. Although I still consider it to be Ronnie's car and am taking care of it for him, I have been taking driving lessons since I do not know how to drive a stick shift. When I can finally drive it alone, the first place I'll go will be to Fort Snelling.

After a good nine months of working on getting the house ready to sell and dealing with everything inside, in summer 2017 Brad listed the house. It was listed around noon on a Monday; that afternoon there were four showings, and six showings were scheduled for the next day. The first showing was at 9 a.m., and an offer that was too good to pass up was made. Brad did a fantastic job, and during the long nine months of getting the house ready, he never pushed to hurry up. Brad helped to make the whole situation much better and easier.

Once everything was taken care of, I wondered what was I going to do. The house was sold, so after the closing I couldn't go over there. It became a time of adjustment. I had to adapt to Ronnie not being here, which was not easy by any means. Before I was busy with the house, but now was the time to deal with the loss.

When Ronnie moved to my house, I told him that the room downstairs that my dad used as an office would be made into his library. We would bring his six bookcases, desk, chair, lamp, table and his knickknacks to furnish "his" room. Unfortunately, it never happened for him to enjoy. Despite his not being here, his library is finished, and I think he would like it. The journal he started writing for one year beginning August 17, 1999, is on one of the shelves. Every evening I go down to the library to read the journal entry for the day. Reading his journal is a comfort and helps to keep him close. At this writing, there is a little less than three months left until the year is finished.

By this time, I have pretty much gone through the highlights of our time together as well as the lower points. There are so many things about our being together that I miss each and every day. One is hearing him call me Annie. He didn't do it often, but when he did it was special. Some years back, he started calling me Tanya. I'm not sure if I have this straight, but as I remember there was a mummy called Caius who said the juice of the tanya leaf would give him life. When Ronnie started calling me Tanya, he said it was because I helped give him life. Nothing could have been more special. He called me either Tanya or sometimes Tany, I sure do miss hearing that. I also miss the feel of his hand on my arm or shoulder or holding hands with him. It is true what has been said that the little things mean a lot. This becomes more apparent when you have lost someone very near and dear to you.

Ronnie's family believed in spirits; mine didn't, as far as I know. After four instances since Ronnie has been gone, I am a believer. The first one happened one night after I went to bed. Lying on my right side, I dozed off for a short time. When I started to partially wake up, I kept my eyes closed, and it seemed very dark. All of a sudden there was a face in front of me, eyes still closed. I tried to stare at it then realized whose face it was – it was Ronnie. I asked, "Ronnie is that you?" After a few seconds, it was gone, and I opened my eyes. The second time started in a similar way, lying on the right side but wide awake when I felt a very gentle pressure, like a very gentle touch, on the back of the left shoulder. Again, I knew it was him. The next time, the cat was lying on the bed on Ronnie's side a little way in front of his pillows. All of a sudden, she started to just stare at the pillows, she kept it up for the longest time. I asked her if Ronnie was there. After a while, she put her chin down on the bed but still kept staring. Another time, again it was at night, and I was in bed on my right side when I heard a voice say "Tanya." That definitely was Ronnie because at that time no one knew he called me Tanya and there was no one in the house other than the cat.

The last instance of knowing Ronnie was with me occurred last fall. The two of us used to go to Mystic Lake Casino. One morning I woke up and decided to go there. We always had a good time there even though we were not big winners. I was at a nickel slot machine, which wasn't doing very much. No one was nearby, so very quietly I asked Ronnie for a little help. After one or two plays, I started winning, then it would stop, and I would ask again and there were some more winners. From there, I went to the quarter machines. Same scenario. Since I had been there close to an hour, it seemed time to think about leaving. Before leaving, though, I decided to try the dollar machines. I tried a couple of them with no luck then went to a 2-coin dollar machine that showed three white sevens on the screen. I thought something like that would be nice. I played two coins at a time. The first two spins did nothing, so I asked Ronnie for a little help again. I told him if I won something, then it would be time to leave. On the second spin after that, playing $2, three white sevens came up on the screen, and I won $400. He didn't fail me. I cashed out of the machine, went to the cashier, and left a very happy player. After instances like these, I had to be a believer.

Despite knowing the end was coming and finally came, there was much that had to be done after Ronnie died. The aftermath became a learning experience. In a way, Ronnie was still teaching me even though he was gone. I had to learn what to do with Ronnie's house and how to get the house ready to sell. Not only did I learn a great deal after losing Ronnie, I learned a lot before his death such as having the strength to care for him as his health declined, trying to comfort him, and letting him know I was there for him and how much I loved him. I guess after everything is said and done what is important is to know you have done everything you could do and you did your best. In the years to come, the idea that you could have done more or could have done some things differently might come up, but by then it doesn't really matter.

Epilogue

I want to thank Boyd Huppert for doing the story about Ronnie for his *Land of 10,000 Stories*. I have the video on a DVD so I not only can hear Ronnie singing but hear him talking and see him smile. Boyd recently did a story about Fort Snelling Cemetery. KARE 11 TV was involved in a fundraising event, Flags for Fort Snelling, to raise money to buy flags to put by each headstone for Memorial Day 2018. I started to fill out the form to donate on KARE's website but was having difficulty since I am not all that good with computers, so I called the station for help. A very nice lady, Janeen, went through the whole form with me and thanked me for donating. I mentioned my husband is there and that I go two to three times a week to have lunch with him. Apparently Boyd, along with some others were discussing his Fort Snelling story when Janeen mentioned what I told her. She said Boyd picked up on it right away. He called me on May 2, 2018, asking if I would agree to be part of the story, as he wanted to interview some who the cemetery meant something to. Absolutely! I met Boyd and David Peterlinz, photojournalist, at Fort Snelling on May 8 for the filming. That evening, Boyd called. He started going through the film finding at least 20 minutes blank and asked if I would do the filming again. We met the following day to redo the filming. Boyd did a wonderful job on the story about the cemetery, which included Ronnie and me. I also have a video of this on the DVD, which means the world to me. It is like the last thing Ronnie and I will do together.

I guess this pretty much winds up our story. Whether it seems kind of strange or it resonates with someone doesn't matter. The relationships couples have are important to them no matter what others think.

As important as the qualities of a good relationship discussed in this book are, the most important quality is love. With a deep, meaningful love between two people, all other qualities should fall into place. I was fortunate to have experienced a love like this spanning 50 years with Ronnie. It grew from a child's admiration to a young adult's developing love to the love of a woman for the love of her life. Even though he is no longer here in person, I know he is always with me, by my side, guiding me through each day. Who could want more?

Rest well, my love, until we are together again.

Photo Album

Ronnie in the 1930s.

Ronnie in the 1930s.

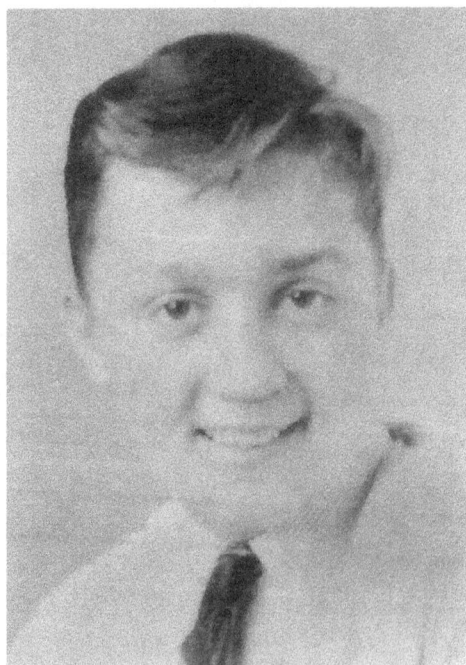

Ronnie's grade school picture.

Ronnie's Chicago grade school basketball team.

Ann in 1947.

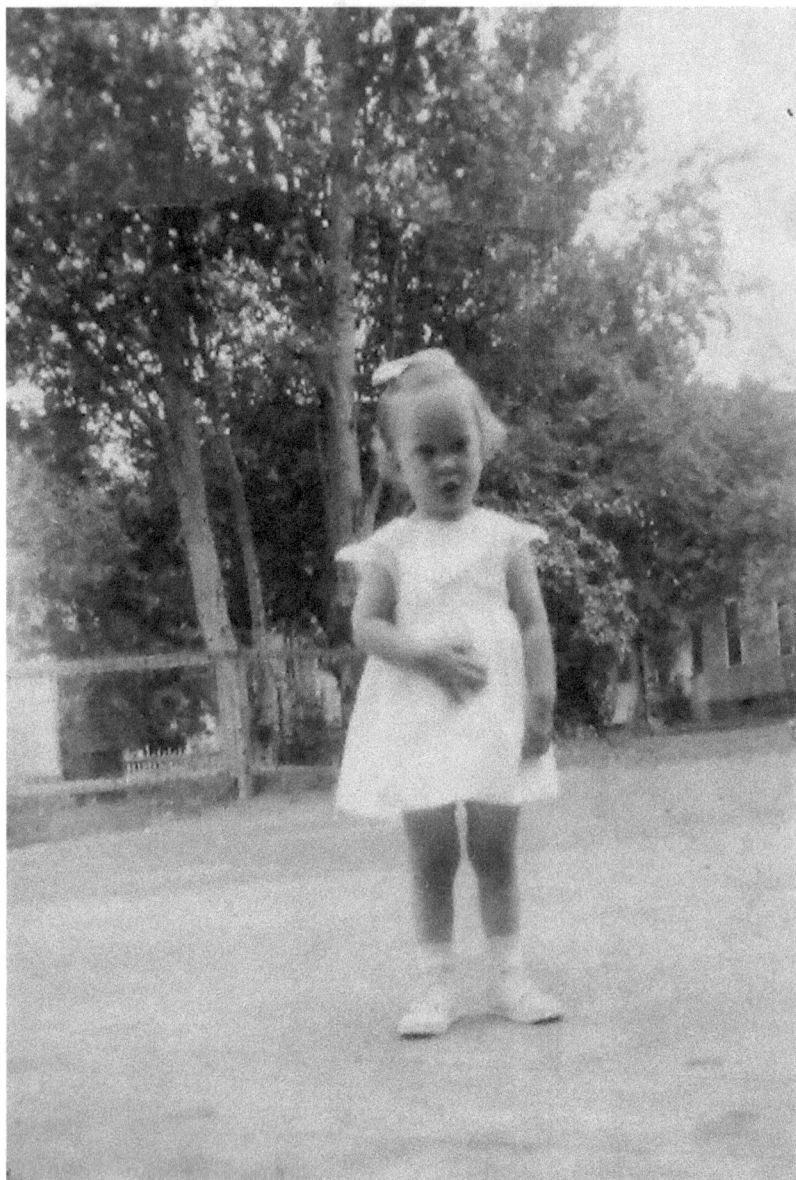

Ann late 1940s.

Ann early 1950s.

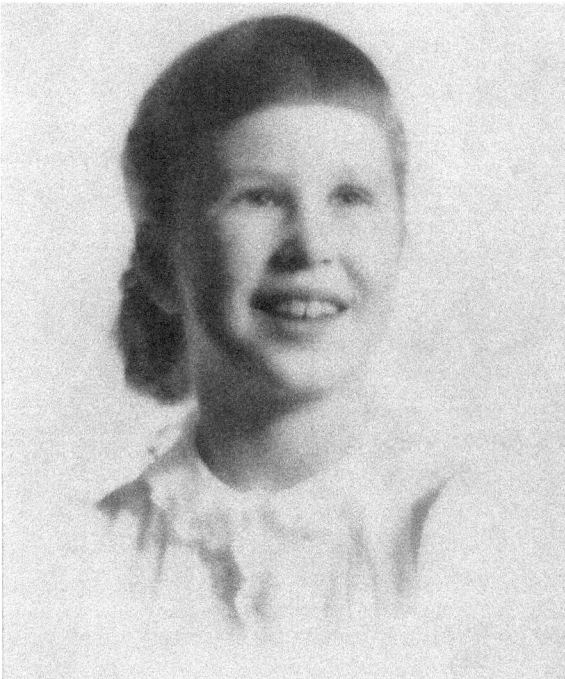

Ann's grade school picture.

Ronnie's high school picture.

Ronnie while teaching at Mechanic Arts High School.

Ronnie's 1965 Corvette.

Ronnie and Ann, 1970s.

Ronnie sporting a country singer look on Cannon River, 1990s.

Marine teddy bear Ann got for Ronnie.

Ronnie, KARE11 reporter Boyd Huppert, and Ann in 2015.

www.ingramcontent.com/pod-product-compliance
Lightning Source LLC
Chambersburg PA
CBHW05055828O326
41933CB00011B/1894